WINE SONGS, VINEGAR VERSES

WINE SONGS, VINEGAR VERSES

BY
HARAMBEE GREY-SUN

Published by HyperVerse Books
www.hyperversebooks.com
writing between and beyond the lines

ACKNOWLEDGMENTS

The author would like to give sincere and humble thanks to the
editors of the following publications in which earlier versions
of some of the poems in this book first appeared:

CrossConnect: "Black Ice"
Reader's Quarterly: "After Mourning"
Wisconsin Review: "A Dinner for Two"

WINE SONGS, VINEGAR VERSES

CONTENTS

TORRONTÉS

Going Out and In / 3

Crosswords / 4

Bedbug Stories / 6

Some May Say . . . And So On / 8

Say Again? / 10

Never Whistle "Whisky" on a Crowded Beach / 12

A Walk in the Dark / 14

RIESLING

Black Ice / 17

Quacksalver / 19

Overexposed / 21

Gaming the Names / 23

The Wild-Child Said: Love Made Me / 25

Patience / 26

Past Harvest / 28

Come Vertigo / 30

ZINFANDEL

Happiness, Kissed / 35

Happiness, Undressed / 36

Happiness, Blessed / 37

Fuck Happiness / 43

A Genesis of Happiness / 45

Happiness, Apocalypsed / 49

Happiness, Lost (Apocrypha) / 51

SHIRAZ

After Mourning / 55

Food—Train—Thought / 58

A Dinner for Two / 60

The Devil's Values / 62

In the Belly of a Sick Fish that Can't Afford to Flush Itself / 64

Self-Reject (assurance for the insecure) / 66

Think Blank / 68

BAROLO

Love, Uninvolved (In Its Own Horror) / 73

Ringed Songs from the Golden Days to Come / 76

Cold Coffee / 78

Winter Away / 80

Impossibly, A Reality / 82

Failing, in the Silliest Business / 84

One Day, For No Clear Reason, My True Love Gave Me a Perennial / 87

TORRONTÉS

Notes:

Elegant; floral bouquet, white peach and layers of citrus; a
balance of sweetness and acidity on the finish.

GOING OUT AND IN

We never do that anymore.
Whenever she asks me to
invite her out for an evening
on the town
for dinner and glancing
at others similarly coupled,
my excuse
is that my eyes and mouth
are exhausted,
so tired from talking to
and looking at . . .
       By then,
she has faded wide away,
entirely uninterested
in what more I have to say.
       And now
the accumulated fades
have produced an inaccurate hate,
(maybe) able to cure a corrupted love
of the cinema, the theater, all of these
and those tragic shows
designed to inculcate desire,
enter-staining the mind
with spiraling blues and greens,
stirring one to envy
sticky figures
stuck in depressing scenes.

CROSSWORDS

At breakfast—every morning,
a similar task—I have to ask, beg over eggs,
for you to please look me in my eyes
and be honest over toast before we part for the day:
me through the garage door, you out through the front.

In the News . . . Forget it, and turn to the Style section,
the word puzzles: How to say *"deception"* in three letters?
A deceptive word and act, you can fill and end it with *"E. X."*
if you refuse to speak with me now.

Questions played—you give one-word replies
preceded and punctuated with a sigh.
"What's the matter? How do you feel?"
"*O. K.*" Two letters. Trivia.
Comments made—"I don't know . . . nothing seems
to fit . . ."—you grunt incomprehensible responses,
And still I hear that you plainly tell your friends
that I never talk, discuss my world with you.
Of course Clara told me.

That note detailing a rendezvous that you found, showed to them,
was composed by one of those confidantes (not me)
to whom you close your eyes and cry
while they laugh
and lie.

Your friends live, love, exist at cross-purposes.
They tried to divide—their way: With one letter,

push U and I away. What do we owe?
Where's this trust, those crossed-heart promises?

How can I know what to tell you unless you talk
and are honest with me first?

"I don't know what bit me,
but one night in bed,
something must've crawled
into my ear; and, well, now
as you see,
it's all swollen."

She heard this then mumbled something that rhymed with *dumb*,
I think, and followed it up with *'cuse*—(the first syllable
was swallowed)—as she quit her breakfast, stood, and turned to exit
out into the too-secluded, variegated garden. I immediately followed
after finishing my danish and coffee, to stand nearby and observe her
searching for something among the hardly-surviving flowers,
and seeming to find answers, afire, from nowhere.
The adumbrated frustration was too apparent.

I honestly couldn't say what was wrong
with her. I warned her not to slake any thirsts with the suspect
water during her week-long trip up north, a one-woman vacation
where, perhaps, she happened upon the worst of all possible worlds.
I was wondering if I should ask her candidly as she continued to grumble—
like thunder before a downpour—about rabbits and their habits ... Never
mind the fact there've never been any vegetables in her garden,
which continued to darken during the morning.

A sun-lunatic, finally run crazy by the cheerless and lazy rays?
Assumption number one. Number two on the list was that something
simply came and went, bumping her in one or a few of the nights she was away.

Was she bug-bitten in attempts to get her smitten until she got wise and spent
her emotions on lotions that could repel the little bloodsuckers and spitters?

That's it, I concluded—she's under stress,
wondering how she should confess to crimes
committed, hopefully, in another state of mind.

I didn't want to push her,
but I was finally forced to ask:
"And what is it that bit you?"

She sighed, rolled her eyes,
reached for the pesticide,
and then replied:
"You don't know?" "No."
"It was something so stupid
it forgot how to swallow."

Apologies expected
to rejoin and soothe over
—but what's the point?

Even she couldn't pull apart what's been stuck
together, massaged with needles—an Eastern treat
to trick runts, the emotionally immature,
kept in a relationship,
stunted.

Some may say it's redundant
to keep sprinkling salts, repeating faults,
tickling the pickled sense with the point
that the sweetness (and so on)
has been going, or is long gone.

Apples pulled down, picked
from the choicest trees, glazed with caramel,
served to houseguests, acquaintances—
same folks who walk through our yard,
take improper glances, whisper to breezes
that aid blazes four properties over.
Who's to blame for the flames?

Some may say something of "karma,"
"just deserts" (and so on), some charming cliché
to explain, to clinch the problem's meaning.

Some may say the sum of our difficulties probably lies
where we lay our energies: in organizing seasonal social gatherings;
our concentration's on hot or cold cider
while too many invitations are sent to outsiders.

Does she accept? Do I regret
letting them into my confidence?
No fences can prevent a Western traveler
in the overrun land of the young sun
after he's unraveled the intricacies of hints of liaisons
experienced during stints for pure pleasure.
Whose business is it?

"I am sorry . . . won't happen again . . ." and so on.
Some may say, "Lies," but it's Truth,
tried and applied: My homegrown method
to make our garden parties more intimate,
the after-talk more interesting,
guaranteed to bring them back . . .
and so on.

SAY AGAIN?

How many times
can I rhyme
Chastity's name
with my favorite things
as a come-on
before she gets up
and pops me in the lips?

The riddle answered,
"Three plus Two,"
before she blew,
"Thank you
for not expecting
something so anti-romantic,
which beautifully shows
I'm not one of those
slow women you've likely known,
who'll stand up, smiling silently
while you say your 'Hi's'
and low lies."

Hell, that's the last time I'll toss my pastime
of trying to cheer this blank-faced woman
out of her obvious fear
of sitting alone
waiting for a long line
to shorten so she may stand, saddened,
to collect her "charity," short
for "charred identity"—a pity

for this smart undervalued beauty—
burned years ago by Jeremy (the germ
of pubescent popularity) and dead-
anxious to earn the wages,
again learn the flavor
of looks licked clean
of personality, perspicacity,
and—*fuck*—any sense of poetry.

NEVER WHISTLE "WHISKY" ON A CROWDED BEACH

"Love—Is that what you do
or just what you want me
to think?"

"You're on the other side of misery.
I just offered to buy you
a drink—"

"Of desert wine, I bet.
I know what comes after
the sweet streams."

An albatross with bum wings caught in-between
a vacationer's insinuations and the weirder actions
of the tide ...
I'd only been admiring the peach-skinned evening,
strolling in loose-tied trunks, green hoodie where the water
tongue-kisses the beach, when I obliviously threw
a whisky-whistle at the blended clouds: mellow,
delicate tones deepening to something more intense.

Simply my show of approval, my nod at a master's piece,
my inspiration and vow to properly embrace and turn
the coming late-hours every which way but tight.
My tweet without letters.

She, passing by, caught it,
dutifully mistaking, taking herself as a woman in peril.

Rather than scream, or flee, she asked me my name,
then began an exchange of sugar water
versus salt.

I would've passed by at a glance, but she insisted I join
a crab scuttle—dancing, bottom-feeding—as if
I'd some ulterior motive she had to read and announce:
He's out to tipple and topple any bimbo he can find
already as plum-red-cheeked as him. It wouldn't be her,
or so she'd declared by yanking, verbally spanking me
in public, yellow-warning any scared others
caring to hear.

While she was nitting and noting,
I noticed her one-piece, wet—*very* wet—clinging tight,
nipples bright, brighter than the weary sun, or
the tardy moon.

My invitation to drinks came too soon, too polite,
too innocent, she never got the leave-me-alone hint,
till the freak-tide's wave snuck up on me, mistaking
my loose trunks.

Talk about plum-red cheeks.

Only an obscurant ramble,

a leggy rant in no hurry—

I followed as closely as one could,

detoured through the tried-and-true routine

of duck-and-dodge, hum-and-nod, stubbing two toes,

rubbing elbows with walking-dead

pedestrian explanations;

casually, a talk through the park turns

into a defense of bums:

"Well, he didn't see the ring . . . It's such a part of me—

'As one,' you know—so I forgot . . . We started talking . . .

Well, what would you have said if you didn't remember . . . ?"

Let's see . . . Start with "Sorry"?

No—that's too near to clear.

Where'd be the adventure?

RIESLING

Notes:

Semi-sweet; zesty apricot, lime, and honey, with floral notes.

BLACK ICE

Tripping over the threshold,
just through the door when
I hear the first ring; can't turn back;
already late for another engagement;
have to let the machine record what it can.

Out to correct the arranger's error:
I ordered red chrysanthemums, not yellow.
During the ride, I'm almost blindsided
by someone whose excuse to the law
would surely be something about a baby on fire.

Errands unending, tearing into the time
set aside to surprise Susan at her office.
Lunch will have to wait; clock, punched to a later date.
Hitting home, finally, I press <play> on the machine:

Pick up. I know you're there. I just passed
and saw your car parked out in front.

Problem—dipping out too early . . . or slipping in too late?
I dial her back for no answer.
Leaving again so soon, I drive to her apartment.
Alternating knocks and rings gets nothing
in response. So I throw up my hands and
drive back, pondering just where Susan might really be.
At a bar with the girls, for a midweek happy hour?
Or, possibly checking who's picked what on the registry?

"She'll ring when she's ready," I decide

as I close my garage door for the final time that night, I swear.

Inside, I glance at the machine and see nothing flashing

as I swing through the kitchen to grab a banana and into the family room

to find, taped onto the television screen, a note, reading:

Selfish, don't forget to let that date at the altar slip from your mind.

Yes, I've discovered what you've been up to.

You'll find your dirty diamond on the mantelshelf,

or maybe someplace underneath.

QUACKSALVER

"This mutual condition of my heart and my head
starts with a glass of the best, the noblest rot,
sweet stream of kisses all the way down the tongue
and esophagus, into the gut, where there's nothing
but knots—bouncing, fluttering mad to unravel
hyper strings—this is my constant instability."

I shut up and glanced about the doctor's office, absent the whining
and wailing of the ER, but dense with smokers' laughs, and jokers'
coughs. I was assured the best specialist for my type would,
of course, set up in the backroom of a bar.

The doctor finished writing, then closed his eyes,
consulting the loyal theories that had stayed since he was robbed
kindly of his license. He smiled broadly, then said:

"Children lie about many things
because they don't know any better.
Adults lie about most things
because they do know better."

"Huh?"

"You're fooling yourself. Forget blaming alcohol;
you will never be fit, right in the mind enough to talk
to an attractive woman without salivating, spitting vitriol
instead of intended compliments. Your lub-dubbing heart
will flick all your words, your hob-throbbing brain will trick
your tongue, while you look like a slobbering degenerate."

He seemed to speak from experience.
"No matter what you want, try to say or might think,
you'll end up fucked."

Well, good—mission accomplished:
I saw a doc about my sweet addiction
and learned it wasn't my problem. No,
my constitution wouldn't allow me to stand
still for one date; impossible for me to process
one place and one face at just one time.
I'd need a new way to stab at relations.

Confidence restored, with a resolution in mind,
I rushed out into the bar, ready to purchase multiple glasses
for multiple women, while winking and asking them
about their space-curving dimensions.

OVEREXPOSED

Out of the blind
Carly approached,
pulled out her own chair,
sat down, unaware
of what would come next—
an open and short discussion
centering on the role
of the high sun
as Chief Liar.

"Kristen saw a photo that seemed to show
something unseemly happening between you and me.
I suspect the mailman of more than just putting it into the slot;
but—" A *SIGH* interrupting (not signing relief),
followed by
*"Aren't you ready to order? This bread's cold.
  Is this cheese or butter?"*
followed by
a meeting of the (pearly) teeth,
a twisting of the (wise) tongues,
a merging of strung words
urging that we—my Kristen and me—reconcile
while, in the distance, I see a younger guy
shaking his fist
at the greying sky.

*"It's only a shot
that should be forgotten,
never remembered."*

"You're not understanding me.
When Kris opened the envelope,
it was as if she'd found the lost shadows of sound.
She hasn't stopped shouting."

Carly doesn't stop eating.
Chewing without swallowing,
she manages to spit out something
about explanations clearing the way
for hearing *"You're forgiven."*

But that picture is far from clear.
And the pic Kristen received, scaring . . .
Staring, one simply sees two blurs
near the heart of the scene
while, in the background, it appears
undead lovers are hovering under a crossed bow,
compromised by too much sun.

Clearly, the only course to freedom from her suspicions
is to conduct my work in darker rooms
wherein some will see the appearance of innocence,
the product of a negative, hardly proven.

GAMING THE NAMES

Strange language:
You always say *"blame,"*
but it never ends with *"me."*

I didn't spit on time,
hit the clock,
knock the box up, yet
I've been rocked, tied, and pulled
into following games with rules
too dense
for common innocence.

Mélange of names untimely played
during our faceless moments of intimacy,
lacing traces of previous relationships . . .
If I'm not bothered by the fact
she was fathered by another man,
then why should you be by my not-yet-committed act
of naming her after one of my estranged ladyfriends?

"I'd rather let her die," I believe,
is a rather extreme reply.

Didn't I offer to pay,
care for the baby as my own?
It's silly to argue over a medley of letters,
pretending a certain combination could turn out to be deadly.
For whom?

In a treacherous bed of noises

unfound in any catalog of sounds,

might it be possible for silence to turn and pronounce us

both, man and woman,

guilty of gambling for treasure we're both sure will pass,

be truly possessed by neither?

nauseous; infectious—Why were we here
two nights ago, all dressed down
to our skintight lunacies?
True love really never dies
is a sick thought that lies
on a bed of gravel, under a sheet
of sleet, traveled over by a sled
we shared, taking turns pulling it
with our clenched teeth.

We're suffering for it, that wonderful
grueling nighttime adventure. Not exactly
"romantic" in the sense of the adjective
I'd grown up knowing and loving, but still—
We were one, alone, cold, needing each other.
Now we're ill, together, in the same naughty spot
making each other sicker.
The thought of this is driving, depriving,
making us lazy.

If we were to simply stand here
in our bare feet, would we contract
the understanding that this is how
honest lovers must live,
act?

PATIENCE

Is a virus
with curative effects
inspiring impure thoughts in a saint
painted with welts (the results
of the plague of the honeybees)?

Charitable rumors passed from ear to ear,
taking a poison-gaseous compassion, making
room for clear speculations in-between:
Walter probably does lead a clean love-life;
he shouldn't be faulted if he's constantly followed,
sometimes swarmed, by ladies
sweet on his reputation.

His refusal to marry too early,
now, or here-soon, was considered yesterday
to be quite rational, quietly inspirational.

"...Wear white for so long, it can't help
but go brown,
or black."

Faint osculations, if combined
into one big moist wind, might find
themselves as that quote, a sentence
thrown in the face—intended to go
on and on, then in,
crawling and winding under the skin—

of a sick, happy, and authentically romantic
possessor of others' lost ticking time.

The wanderer handed the teller his note:
"Crisp, clean, random-numbered
leaves, untraceable—What's my face
telling you?" The teller rolled her eyes,
clicked her tongue without alarm, ready
to charm with her green-and-whites
this hobbling fool in her parlor.

Unable to speak, cursed to write only poetry,
he'd arrived with colored bandages—Indian summer's
subtractions—wrapped smartly around his head.
This barely walking, non-talking torture, he
wanted a fortune, an ensured happy ending.

It would cost nothing less
than a charred piece of his heart.

But the traveler had already torn
and worn himself beyond destitution, his
fevered destinations pulling him through
all the wrong seasons; he'd been strung up
and wrung by Eden's vines (implanted in him)
and bent through Heaven's hypercubed dimensions.

Fate, slaked: Forever through his veins, ice
wine would flow, reminding constantly, forcing
him to be sweetly pleased with his worst mistake:

Waiting to approach his would-be bride
far too late.

COME VERTIGO

In illness or in Hell—
that's the choice?
What else but the enigmatic stigmas
placed on those laced in love—
can't eat; can't sleep; but keep
throwing up; too tired, unable
to push back from the table
and dwell on anything, anyone
else.

The mark of the smitten bachelor:
Trip-circled. Away with the other
would-be bees seeking what's mine.
(Relationships are for sweet suckers.)
Repel further those who might interest me
if only I were healthy enough to see clearly.

The mark, traced around my eyes, down,
on the chest (off-center?), around and
—what's surrounding me? Lovers or enemies?

All too common, this community of conspirators,
perspiring to tip the scales,
pay and push the balanced man away from his spiced life, out of
the unsure labyrinth featuring various teary-eyed teases at every turn,
into secure chains, wedded to the promise to work work work
at all problems. Real, or (probably) imagined. Robbed of rest,
sold into the slow burn.

Lost freely in misery,
or given to last in—I was told—
a golden (honey-coated) slavery?

Well, society is pushing me . . .

ZINFANDEL

Notes:

Intense; crushed raspberries and blackberries, cracked black and white pepper.

HAPPINESS, KISSED

[Mani's lament]

"I wish you Happiness,"
 I wrote by candlelight,
"'preciate the invitation,
 but don't think I can make the flight.

"I wish you a slow life
 beyond the exchanged vows."
Her invite smelled of old perfumes,
 scents to which I'm allergic now.

Signed my last words with "Love."
Postscript: "Excuse the smears.
Fought to keep my hand steady, but
ink tends to run when kissed by tears."

HAPPINESS, UNDRESSED

[Mari, post-ceremony]

Why should I be so pleased to receive
the several flavors I never asked for?
This apple-candy
cocktail is simply
nothing more
than transmuted wails.

The cold and crackling road to this reception:
Favors risked and paved over
by deranging parents;
culture picking at an undead infant.

"Unpleasant" is too meek and mild for
such a wild embrace in the unspeakable
white heat, too tall, coercing—futilely—
the slaves of love
to keep
its pungent ashes polished.

Such a slave-driven wish only makes sense
to those wrapped in paper traditions,
smothered in the fragrances taken on
by backward glances, never much bothered
by the real scents of men,
the true sense of women,
or the honest touches
of whim.

HAPPINESS, BLESSED
[Mani, tipping through the garden]

Simply
a bump
in the night's
road
to wherever
careless days
lie
and shiver—

Is that
all
I've been
seeing
through her
torn-curtained
and dusty,
window?

Them,
in the bedroom,
screaming.
In the tulips,
me,
on the other
side
of a pane,
the prodigal
son

of dawn,
muttering
the only
pitiful
ditty
I can—
Light-bringer's.
Laughed at,
an outcast
sworn to,
then scared
from his
sacred
duty.

Some of us
(like flies
on feces)
attract
enemies
simply
because
we exist.

She,
my would-be
Love,
perpetually
attracted
the rough
and ready,

and smiled
at the
nastiest
and
rudest
triple-
dipping
opportunities.

I'd declined
the polite
invitation
to see her
wed
the rudest;
but, now,
watching
this bastard
of ceremony,
wasting
his unearned
Happiness,
I can not
help
but want
to
intrude . . .

Hell,
I could be
wrong,

seeing
things,
bitter,
itching
to belt out
a
belated
wedding
tune.

A bump,
a slap—
or welcomed
love-tap?

Her very
breath,
each
and every
particle
of her
raw speech
steams
the room,
fogs
the glass
as she
spits
passion
into
his face—

in-
between
hers
getting
rosier
and rosier.

The hiss,
this Happiness,
whoever's—
it's clearly
Bliss,
hot
and heavy
Heaven.
The one
I still
desire.
I simply
need
a song,
transmuting,
unleashing
a legion
of flies
with lassoes
to crawl
over her
lesioned
body,
capturing

her
to ask,
simply:
"Are you,
True Love,
ready
and set
for me,
yet?"

FUCK HAPPINESS
[Mari's gethsemane]

It's over
the crystal slush of time's remains:
A squeeze of lemon angels,
a twist of orange demons
employed to help
push the dawn all the way down.

Vodka Buddha—
my breakfast joy—my brilliant ploy
to eliminate the self
and the one
golden-ringed to me. Mercy-kissing off
this acidic light-eater. This is the only
arrangement I've been allowed
to have a say in since
my Caesarean, my own
séanced birth.

Others say
a true whore would fuck Happiness
and give legitimate change
while accepting counterfeit currents
through her veins
and nerves, deranging
the brain, remaining the same.

I say a true heart, enraptured in vain,
feels it's not God

but man
that is mad at Satan
because Satan chose God
      over man,
the Essence of Love
over the fleshy
      second-hand
      creator
      of bloody hate.

. . . but the joke's on Jack Spite;
this whole holy whore
      of a man
who has the religious courage
that coarsens the skin, traditionally
irritates the soul, has caused me
to crash and laugh and stumble-
bumble my entire being
into prohibited territory—
the irradiated land of Eve's stories.

      I'm growing,
developing a fear of flowers. "Honey,
let's not talk about fruit tonight,
only concoctions, conceptions,
receptions." Deceptions. He gave
the names to his animals, within.
      I'll give
five minutes of fame to the cannibals
seeking intoxicated Eve's revenge.

A GENESIS OF HAPPINESS
[A proposal: Mani versus Mari]

So, you've been watching me?
An eye-rhymer without reason . . .

I've been encompassing
harassment,
trying to squeeze it
into compassion.

A creepy ex-boyfriend,
with no girlfriend
or any other friends—
Why shouldn't I
call the authorities?

Why didn't you
call them on your husband?

Just dust. You mistrust everything,
subsisting on stale air, fattening
yourself on juvenile fantasies.

My dreams of when you and I were young,
it's true, they chitter-chatter at night
like our teeth now, under these afternoon clouds—

Stuttering jokes, while drooling, some
idiots' mist—

Heaven's crystal fortresses fellated by tongues
of flames, criss-crossing-curses
rehearsing for the days
of divorce—condensing Paradise.

I refused to wait
to be raped by Fate.

You chose instead to cut off
Adam's lub-dubbing head.

You probably watched it all,
you—a moon-clocking stalker.

Couldn't be helped.
It was a slumping triumph of spectacle—

Like you, a weird, once-wordless third man,
out and about, criss-cross-cruising
the shadows tossed away by every pebble
and stone on the narrow two-way lane
through the weeds, trying to scatter, plant
sour apple seeds in our retarded garden.

I needed a hobby. Flowers, vegetables . . .
You should have been growing escapes
on vines, strangling Adam's dreams, while
I tilled the plot hoping to cultivate the new fruit:
a blues drawberry—with each bite, you'd be able
to erase and re-illustrate, rescuing yourself:
the lost bride of Jekyll.

You're only heckling me, circle-joking
on the spot-on killing of my husband.

A nice murder in the ice of blurbled passion,
choked up on the coldest, drunk-plunken words.
Leave him buried; let me pass and carry you beyond—
here—into your revamped garden . . . We—the light-bringer
and the coarse singer—with the soul potential to see and saw
the azul foil above, rip, fail the sun's common light,
and fool each particle, up from two children's crushes—
us—freed, mutually seeing ourselves, divided, sliced—
atom by atom from the passions pulsing in every fruit and herb,
rock and clod, blade of grass and leafy shield, each and every
crossing, engaging in an everlasting battle, it seems, between
true Love and the wounded world. Each part of us, bursting,
won't be gem, just a droplet, each one of a different color
depending on how Love's eye meets whim's lens.

Heh. Circle-joking again.
I've surely been beaten,
but you're clearly abused
by the assumption I would tear
my self, my soul apart
merely for you.

Purely for Love,
run away with me—your soul,
your self, already sown
to the air—this war, generalized
by desire and delirium. Acknowledging

what's really the matter would allow
you to hack the limbs free, for starters.

I no longer have a heart.

You have pain, radiating, another form
of light. Dark energy, dark matter, and dark
musick—I'll take you slow, reverse the collisions
of compromises, the collusions of dead decisions,
and take you back to the beginning of our first kiss.
We'll gaze at each other, younger, re-experience
how we felt, and just simply deal with it.

Up from crushes, dust of infatuations
drained of reason, irrational roses—

They exist, as will we, as fragrant
vagrants in the lost-and-restored
Creator's new Creation.

Your memory's not what it used to be—
but, hell, let's see
what we can see.

HAPPINESS, APOCALYPSED
[Mani's fate]

Pain ensured and endured from a first kiss
blessing the last fear, dismissed from the brain, passed
to the heart, where it turns and ties those wormy feelings.

No stomach necessary to experience the mess
Love's germs makes of one's organs, orgasms, and senses.

Sent through Synesthesia, flayed by the same flickering lips
that assaulted Heaven's promises: What a gauntlet! What'd I get
for my trouble of trying to help a lost woman? Suspension,
desiccated body in flowing greens
of praying layers, stalling walls, and screens
of photogenic muses' sick.

This body, my world of spy-wires for hire
to the lowest moral bidder resulted out of conflict
between lust and phosphorus; shallow breathing,
feeding that brain scooped from then stuffed into the chest:
tomato—potato—hunk of coal with crystalline
tendrils, writhing, winding, sending chills, further
rending the flesh, reading the black texts
on Love's philosophies and teasing the earth,
pushing me to birth my self, my soul
out of my own mouth. A fruit-and-vegetable-
and-tuber giant of the air and soil, consuming desire,
drooling acid, chiding the body
for what it's hiding—that mistaken, baked contagion:
apologetic sin.

This is Love. Its demise, my surprise;
or my demise, its. Fully realized with a kiss,
single, I die—seemingly, eternally.

Mari sought to feast, detox, rehabilitate
her ability to retaliate against Happiness;
thus, she supped on my body, sapped my spirit
as it spiraled and wafted to heights where clouds
would form, reign, and throw mighty shadows,
shows of lights, bowing. Forgetting
rings, she could've had her own new,
unnamed realm rivaling the toy-
collecting Destroyer's.

Instead—dyed bride—she made me into
a hybrid monster representing every
other man that made a gift of himself,
and nothing more.

This is Love, misplaced. This is Hell, disgraced.
Me facing me. Skin wind-whipped, peeling, inner-
gnawed, flaking, ultrasensitive and taking in
all of this world's offerings—soil, dust, and air;
despair, distrust, and a failing hope
of returning what the world's missing:
the open, enclosing, embracing Honesty
of Us—just Us.

HAPPINESS, LOST (APOCRYPHA)
[Mari, tripping through Eden]

Out of the corner of your lies
sweeps a shade,
a sky-blue shade
—or is that baby blue
and black?—blowing
nos, nevers, here-
evers, and other clever
ways
to be
free
of me
seeing
a sleazy felicity.

My easier Happiness tried
and denied
of travel and leisure, hunting
truer treasure: venison, real meat
over vermin—you—the too-
real man who confined
slutty-slutty me
(as you would say, and indeed
have shouted) while I would fly
or try
and fail
into a dance
unintelligently
designed—a clear function,

but no purpose, slapping about
in a muddled mind. Five-dimensional
seven-limbed chimera climbs
out of it: feathers, purplish flesh,
fish scales and all these/that/those
crap-sappy petals.

They say red and brown flowers
would be lovers of the world.
I say simply to the bumblebees,
"You buzzers got the plight right."

SHIRAZ

Notes:

Complex; black forest fruits, dark chocolate, and subtle vanilla.

AFTER MOURNING

A wake
after sleep-swept words
kept and taken
even on the rawest of rarities,
you knew,
you know it's inevitable
that the suns of war
dry up
after the downpour
of low noons.

So smart, to reteach nature,
we each whispered cruelties
into the other's ear
after sipping
Girl Grey tea.
Temporarily bedded,
we dipped our lisps
into deeper voices
to titillate, to arouse
(to mutilate whatever children
left in the house) for foreplay.
Oh? And what was it
you didn't say?

The sunny conceit
of lunar deceit, as if
one and only
may have what's left

of the right
to deceive December
into a realm of flowers,
trees, and bees. Unheard birds
and dead butterflies rest, floating
down the river of sticks.

Constructing
with the wooden naughty bits:
broken pieces
of once promising friendships
selling,
sold,
sailed
off for a play, staged
on that world-famous
Ocean of Devotion.
What? Were those tears
supposed to tear me away
from the part
I was destined to take
and pull me back
into a pale relationship?

Parting gift for the actor
before the show blows on:
Twelve dead roses—*There,*
since you're so in love
with sinful symbols.

Yes, it's the same hung story,
acted out,
its lines sung
under yet another name.

I went through this in bed,
why should we backtrack now—
just so you can catch a cow under a half-moon?
If you couldn't stand under a cloudless midnight,
then how can it be better expressed over a hot bowl
of breakfast mush? With buttered croissants and milk
to wash it all down . . . What fresh clarity did you expect?

Well, no matter what meal, I can tell you—for real—
I caught dinner and a flick with two *male* friends.
Call them; inquire. Try to call them liars,
steam engines switched to the wrong tracks.
They'll rail down parallel truths, the details of the movie, too.
I'd tell you, but my cereal's getting cold.

Your black coffee, too.
Finish . . .
              Push away that pinkish, acidic pulp.
Drink. You'll need to be alert enough to care,
to think when on the road with the sleepy bears in their cars
on your way to work. You don't want a wreck to interfere
with your morning meeting at the watering hole . . . ?
Perhaps the nature of the gossip gathered at that station
will give you sufficient evidence to reverse your convictions.

Although it's improper to say at the eating table,
I should warn: you may hear something about a fable named "Goldi"
and her invitations to three men at once. Don't believe it;
it's to deceive stable wives trusting enough to let

their men [from the chains to] have a [gang's] night out.

Don't ask me why they might say ... I don't know; crazy motives away:
flushed through the body, leaking pipes, cooked sewage ferts the grounds;
mundane beans sunned among tropical shrubs, up comes a nub of a beanstalk;
through a bleak white fragrant field walk migrant workers jazzed into their minds,
picking madder cherries and carrying off ...

Yes, I know that's mixed sense—
I could tell you a tunnel of truth
you'd be free to think through,
but, if I do, I'll miss my train.

A DINNER FOR TWO

Since she excused herself
to visit the sink and mirror,
the waiter has been waiting, refusing
to bring out our food. Starved, pissed, and
cursed with an abundance of sensitivity, I,
my ears (uncontrollably) search for, feast on
the most unusual conversation pieces
and bits:

"... and right at the point
when he's thinking *What's the point?*
that's when you turn the burn around
and ask him to dance ..."
"... that's the last time
I dedicate my first album to a tramp
who still won't go lower, only blowing me
kisses and best wishes ..."

Sinking. Ill. How else can one feel
ingesting others' guttered utterances, skillfully seasoned
with the right verbs, making the intangibles edible
and irresistible? (Damn—How long does it take
to clean a contact lens?) Soon, I'll be thinking
in tongues, dwelling on so many dumb-blows:

"... oh, purely in form
for one born of a worm,
worn-through with acidic ideas—the bum
actually referred to kids as 'the fleas of marriages' ... !"

"...what was cute about her before
is now just irritating—CUT IT OUT!—
you know? Pure ignorance personified ..."
"...between you and me, I just couldn't stand
to remain across from him, sitting,
being coerced to happily stare at
or avert my sight while he chews with his mouth open;
much of the appetizer is still on his shirt ..."

Sated—Having their fill, my ears give their gift
to my eyes (famished) as I look in the dimmed direction
of this last voice, familiar, in time to see my date
seeing her way to the door—fast.

Staring—Who else is blessed to appreciate
the sight of a child, skipping
the main course, being force-fed
arid desserts as his mouth remains empty
and shut?

Stoned—Hector, sard-hearted errorist actor,
assumes some soft good may come after
sacrificing himself
in the name of roses.

How else should he fight for, take his freedom
but play dead? Hector now only knows he never should
have gotten out of her head.

How could one, two afford to sleep (counting themselves out
as sheep) a week before a wedding in which one of them has a part?
When Juan—that *"poor old friend"*—appeared, she probably forgot
to play Not-to-Get, the flirty song-game, loud and bound to drown
out any heart, murmuring—not worth hearing.

Hector picked up, continued counting to zero,
to the core, by asking her: "Why?" She, though excited,
easily recited: *"A mad poet made me do it."*
He fought back his pure reply: "Sure.
The faithful devil that you know well,
Infidel."

Instead he only nodded, biting aplomb—Holey apologies, wholly
unfulfilling, not fooling those who buy, spend, deal with inhuman feelings.
Is she, he wondered, one of those who's still-and-forever in love with
the unavailable, willing to be convenience's slave, imagining a future
father's birth, not worth having?

. . . No; what followed was too melodramatic

for his thoughts, thankless preoccupations not worth saving
in any reputable bank—as if any institution would accept them.

Hector abhors murder;
so the only clear option left open to him is to stay straight,
marrying his near-perfect fiancée (forgiving her little mistake)
while remaining faithful to his Mistress, five months pregnant,
as he sincerely believes not one of the three
is worth leaving.

IN THE BELLY OF A SICK FISH
THAT CAN'T AFFORD TO FLUSH ITSELF

"You're lucky I ever even looked at you"
is not what Jonah wanted to hear
on his blind date, twenty-second in a series
of serious disappointments, boring glass-apple
stories, robbed of even a moral at the core.

And this latest was off to such a promising start,
from his suggestion they meet for pre-supper coffee,
cherry tarts, and ice cream, to shaking hands—no hugs—
pulling out her chair, and beaming mere-mortal adoration
of her list of endless talents, recited at a hummingbird's pace
before the first cup was even poured. Twenty minutes in,
she asked about him, his hobbies, his passions—right about then
his lips flipped, slipping up his words.

Nerves already twitching, it probably wasn't a good idea
to prod them with caffeine before courageously attempting
to calm himself with the chocolate straight-from-the-freezer
cream that numbed his tongue and set his teeth chattering
as he blathered on and on about his love of cherry tarts, his skill
as a marksman, the pounds he could squat, and his unending passion
for Kant.

Apparently appalled by his stutter-mumbled philosophy,
with plum-sized eyes, she accused him or it: "Disgusting!"
"Immature!" "Pervert!" "I can't believe—!" He didn't understand
where she was coming from, but he knew the destination:

I now mispronounce you
boyfriend and girlfriend.

He was content in the knowledge some would never know
anything that stood beyond the bounds of their own experience;
but he failed miserably to understand why he could never comprehend
his own awkward words. The space and time in his mind
only made sense in the realm of a different species.

But as she rose, he tried to recover: "When I saw you, I thought for sure
my luck had changed." Clearly untrue, based on the cruel and unusual
laughter he inspired: Just a quip about his luck as she whipped back
her braids, grabbed her jacket, turned, and stomped for the door.

Jonah sat still, shivering, smoldering,
wondering how he could reasonably rest forever
in the dark without ever even experiencing
more than just a hint of a spark.

SELF-REJECT
(assurance for the insecure)

So, as a private service, he—no, I don't have a light—
he asked you not to give in, dive into your satisfactions?
He proposed you just sit on,
in the theoretical field of unified lies,
lied on, laid on, agreed upon by the greedy?

In those words?
Ignore him . . . that insensitive ass.

What? No, I haven't seen, but I've heard about that menu
(minus the wine list) where it's written that I must cater to you,
serving you only delicacies (sweetie, meaty, and spicy),
and when you've had your fill, begging your pardon to have a portion.

Sure, I'll excuse you while you go freshen (it'll be a relief);
I'll do my best to find something to amuse me while awaiting

your friend? I'm sorry; I'm sure we haven't, yet.
. . . And you . . .
what did you say?
Oh yes, of course it's the truth (I guess)—you're her true friend,
could never exist in the wrong, neither in words nor in actions.
Who cares what they say, do. Whose side are they on? For you?
Then defend until they (you) perish . . . the thought: blank. Checked it.
Fill in your own name.
I'll do it. For you:
Nice meeting—

66

Good; you're back. We were just discussing the "My Baby" Philosophy.

Yes, it's as innocent (immature) as it sounds;

superhumanly (as possible) strengthened by popular perceptions of weakness

(and winked at by the little ones themselves), constant wails,

demands and grabs for equality in society, while at cozy level, reacting

to phantoms, stabbing and jabbing to defend the defaulted position of superiority.

What?

I didn't mean anything by it. No, I'm not being mean.

Didn't I already say that I was sorry once tonight? OK, I'm sorry.

Again. Yes, I know we can't fight. In public: the eyes; the impressionable.

It's not in fashion (hot) among the (cool) young ones.

But don't worry.

One day, you'll grow up, away from all that.

I'm sure soon after you'll meet your desired match.

THINK BLANK

We are weak echoes, made flesh,
from a Ghost's last shouted wish.

Sheryl clearly guessed life's meaning
as this answer to another query
gassed through her
on a hazy Monday morning.

With intuitively-gathered
and well-sharpened fun facts,
she could easily puncture
boyfriend Ted's toytime theory:

We're just forgotten playthings
of a Child
who grew up
to be a blind and senile
Watchmaker

which takes a feeble, febrile idea
and kids it
with white nights, red clouds,
and pink noises—distracting effects
to make it seem wonderfully original.

A know-it-all who knows everything
that sits on the level
swinging just above "Nothing,"
Ted's not annoying enough to ex-out

or significant enough to hate,
but he rests at about the right position
where Sheryl could always comfortably say,
"I'll just ignore him,
this time."

Now enlightened, she wonders
if "I can create a blank space
to stuff his future bluffs in"—a dustbin
for all the pretentious wise statements
he's sure to make.

She stares, unblinking,
at the invisible waves of pink noise
until she freaks out, thinking
she sees the broken bodies
of dolls,
and mad little boys.

BAROLO

Notes:

Dense; black cherry, violets, leather, and smoke.

LOVE, UNINVOLVED
(IN ITS OWN HORROR)

What if, when you die, you get stuck
in one of your old dreams?

Like the knotty one where you
keep telling me, "There's so much
I'm not telling you"?

I'm thinking of us at City Hall,
combined,
dancing—

With four sinister feet . . .

The best citizens lined up in a parade
to gawk, and grin, and hear
me
serenade you.

Hear me
say a prayer:
God, excuse
their grins.

Me, in black; you, in off-white.
We don't want to show off
anything too bright.

Anything enters Everything, spits out
Nothing to do with your empty-ball fantasy.
Mine's of the past: If only an ear had fallen
off during the third act
of fucking
hacking
heckling the entire art form,
we'd both be better off. You,
in touch with cold reality. Me,
not wasting my warm breath.

They'll all consider us hot-lucky—
you and me, the type to go out
from the town, plucking peaches,
picking cherries, choosing—

The eyes from mimes, while
they're love-faking, taking
the time of their cheery lives.

I'll work, run errands, sing
sweet nothings till the day
you lie back and conceive . . .

You've got to be kidding me; I'm
crying: Douse the damned muse!
Put her on the fucking pyre,
for making me sick.

We'll forever stick together, never argue,
grow old and gray, ever closer . . .

The words that I say and have said, however
I've said them, may as well be glass-eyed dead.
Clark, here—he clearly can't hear—
is a perfect specimen of that special man
who, when speaking to his once and would-be
lover is speaking only to himself, debating
negation. I have a dream . . .

Indulge me . . . just one last time.

Yet another origin of a boy
without a mind, only a brain made up
of an orgy of gray worms, words that matter
less than the body decomposing at my feet.
He'd never listen nor let me go, so
I stuck the stem into his dreamy eyes
and rose from the occasion. He can't exist;
but he still insists on wishing us together.

RINGED SONGS FROM
THE GOLDEN DAYS TO COME

"Let us live now on impulse;
why shouldn't we run and raze some wisdom,
that city under the dome of stained ice,
pretend the raindrops are the customary wild rice?
Let them speak dumbly of freedom
and other bum notions too drunk, numb to stand;
our nonworking, smirking circle of false friends
can continue to stalk with words while sitting still."

Clever Betty will never set her sunny urgings
despite knowing we are already linked irreversibly
by lead rings, unseen, submerged beneath our skins.
She only thinks an official offer, unsaid
(actions unaccompanied by words), may undo
the curse that came a year before the first act's anniversary . . .

"Let us undress, lie down on black light,
teach each the lessons of achromatic mothers
whom we'll finally be able to read through
the expressions of their Dawn-daughters, every morn.
Let them be born into Evermore—
a tale of fairies, unburied, emerging from icy tombs,
iron wombs, into our dark-harmonious real lives."

Sever Betty from her silver-soul (dangerously reflective—
Keep looking deeper within until self-infected
with sweet winged thoughts that sing while rotting the brain)
and she may come to sanely believe

even if we engage and get married, it won't erase

the miscarriage of our twin sons from history.

How else can I convince her they're not resting

in an alternate realm just a few frozen threads away,

in an undead sea-sky?

COLD COFFEE

Intending only to drop off a story sobbed dry
of more than memories, I arrived at evening,
and arose to leave on the dawn
of erased promises of freedom:

A one-sentence premise of several one-act plays
all under the heading of "Adultery,"
the reviews of which, of course, led to divorce,
separating me from a son, twelve years young
and already delving into the worship of dust
—the past.

Our recent ritual, every Saturday, starting at noon:
A repast of bread and blood, semi-relaxed exchanges,
reposing questions that ask about regrets, and whether
I should have let the woman with periwinkle irises pass
without pausing. . . . can only guess that Heather, my estranged,
put him up to this.

I could attempt to blame a coffee-stained mania,
the aftereffects of which forced me to stay awake, then still,
lying like a passive lake pondering a name-change.
Making blood from honey—The vain result of stirring her hair,
playing unfairly, sharing early chocolate through an afternoon
of diversions reversed. I've been there;
and I fear he'll arrive.

No matter what apologies or explanations I offer,
he'll only see a mad-at-wife, dead-to-life, unbothered father

whose single lesson to his son is that, when he's old enough,

being a man means one must maintain a conscience

like a clean

and half-full glass

of cold coffee.

In blemished memory of myself: A widowed father,
one late morn in October, (half past sober)
wrestling for a story with the inner narrator
(or, the rat that ran backwards)
who, achieving victory, proceeded to relate a tale
only a sixteen-year-old would believe,

take to heart, accept as a great reason for an only-child
to depart from home. Like her mother
(I fear), she's destined to get lost in the parti-colored mists
while being drawn toward a myth of clear fire.

Tried, but too tired to hold this slurred version of the story back:
      A teenager, led to run away,
      turned young-adult streetwalker,
      converted into a homemaker
      who, one early evening, in her car,
            met an unlovable drunk,
      resulting in a dead body at roadside.

. . . Now, not sure those occurrences
were experienced by the same person.
Maybe it was just a convenient chore:
clichés clutching each other,
holding on for a dear wife,
while leaving reality, believing only in themselves.

When, in our word-war, she heard me tell (yell at) her that
"You'll end up just like your mother!"

which lone line in that old dog's tale did she take, tug,
in order to be pulled away?

The white lies that find two, tie
and bind, stronger than the sky-blue glue of truths,
it seems, for some insane reason, stay clean
only when read silently.

IMPOSSIBLY, A REALITY

Across the sandy eyes of fantasies,
seven years, tearing, severing families,
comes crawling an infant
under the skin,
nick-picking at stitches to itch,
re-open after scratching what the Raiser
cut on an outspread blood-blue blanket.

Who could've believed, or even guessed,
a male discovering self, obsessed with sex,
at the age of thirteen would back away from an older woman's
flirtations, advances in the name of a sly science, played
like a mountain game in which the hiker's waylaid
by an aunt promising nothing more
than a homemade meal in the open air?

Yeah, plenty of use to, at the age of twenty,
now accuse her of what's lately termed "abuse"
that would've, should've been inappropriately appreciated
by one who once told a couple of cousins of images
(in mind) where sin skins kin. I'd simply be seen as
giving a skewed version of a familiar story with a screwy plot—
In other words, telling it like it's not.

Gazing so long into a cracked mirage until what emerges
is a confusion of intent and consent, squinting back
at the looker, making him crazy enough to start

seeing voices,

hearing colors,

tasting odors

of pre-adolescents: Proof of relations produced,

born of the Seducer, bearing names bound to be traduced—

but, tradition conditions. How can I claim violations and be heard?

"They ask for it in their actions, not to mention their words."

Near the heart of liquid matters,

hands try to reach while speech stays dry.

FAILING, IN THE SILLIEST BUSINESS

"How do you know you're really a man?
I mean, really know?" Genes, and jeans, and
Jeanne all say one thing; but here is Kelly,
questioning the plays I've made with my body
on hers.

Or is she merely being cheerfully metaphysical,
trying to burst the typical mental picture
of cloudy-blue-eyed,
blonde-tressy
secretaries?

After a fifteen-minute flight, lying ragged like a kite
hit by lighting, I was fizzed shy, sneezing, frisked
by *"Anyways . . ."*—the ambiguous ending
to a small dusty fling, one that started in the office
when I openly admitted I was scared of kites,
the heights they sometimes reach—twisting, tumbling
in those fierce winds, the minute constituents
of face-eating pollution, and the too-dark-to-be-bothered
rumors of electrical storms.

Kelly found my phobia silly and sufficiently cute,
or so she said when she came to hand off an envelope
in the mailroom; one exchange rearranged for a better
—or so I thought until flashing-blue struck.

With her, I experienced something never before felt,
not even with my beloved Jeanne, the first assurance

of my masculinity. The second assurance—my son—
has yet to manifest. So I'd curled my fingers around
a friendly risk, and shook it like the knotty limb
of a forgotten enemy. I didn't care to know
the physics of wet string entangling wood
undoubtedly rotted by unseen fungi.

"Blondes have more fun only in their heads,"
was the best comeback I could think of in defense
to what may have been, not a rumination, but a warning.
An intended hour of two illicits funny-tumbling around
turned sour, sadly—quartered hearts loving nothing
but the sweet idea
of finally coming apart.

I knew what awaited us once we both returned
from our mutual sick day: A murder of crows,
gossipy, who know of nothing better to do than peck
and pick and stick their beaks into everyone's business,
to sip and speak of it then, now, and later over the carrion . . .

I'm overthinking,
thinking over this conductive seductress who's suddenly
back on top of me, overwhelmed already by the shuddering
nits mercy-kissing me all over. A second wave of frisson,
a rash decision:

Kelly wasn't a real woman; the lie was in her name;
she bent genders and threatened to break up my marriage,
break my promise to my true love to give her our son. Mine

was a crime against an animal; give it three thoughts—it's silly.
I did the only thing a real man could.

ONE DAY, FOR NO CLEAR REASON, MY TRUE LOVE GAVE ME A PERENNIAL

"Again, I'm sorry;
can't I begin so simply—?"

He could and he did
two years ago, at the metro
bus stop, under the dying blue when:
"I was only going to ask about your openness
to receiving a roommate, different—I assure—
in looks from me, and even gender, but the same
in name. My sister is looking for a place to stay
while she—" *I stopped him, then, distracted*
by something I initially hated but that belatedly
attracted me: that piercing, the signature
in this city, of a certain type of man-
boy.

He saw me squint, probably got the stupid hint;
consciously—smartly—I intended to quit my cover
and quickly move on, hop away, hoping only to hear
him behind me say: "Love the green contacts, thanks
for not flashing mixed signals." *But the bus came,*
and stopped. We boarded, and talked shop.
He was in law school; I was a senior paralegal.
I knew I could teach him some behind-the-scenes tricks
he could use in his power-bright future. It might sound crude,
but I saw in him one whose moral core I could refill.

We stepped off the bus together, under a downpour.

87

Way past apologies, I see the pest of psychology:
cheaters chat, bragging about and regretting
what they should've never done, but would gladly do again.
I admitted to Agnes. Her face wiped itself blank, then
when she rose, it stained to a pinot noir, brow
furrowed, mouth open, ready to throw invectives,
or so I suspected (knowing all too well the amazing
process of how sweet unsure come-ons are sourly translated
into bold courageous put-downs); so I tried to cut
the head off of spurned-spite's body
by twisting, reversing, and slightly modifying
a two-year-old invite: "I presume you prefer loneliness,
rather than having to perpetually split
the late rent, the spoiled food, the disappointments, between two.
I can be out of here by tomorrow, noon." Agnes said something
about the Law of Distraction and the Rules of Contractions.

I neither understood nor saw
what she touched when she reached
into her open robe's pocket, just as
I heard a tapping, and then a rapping.
The "*Someone's at the door,*" was muttered
while she puttered to the door, a rhythmical shuffle
that skipped and tripped into a scuffle.

I turned and hurried into the next room,
and almost slipped on the oil-stained cherrywood.

*I scratched that bitch's eyes out. It was funny how quickly
everything flowed, how swiftly it spilled. The regretted admissions,
voided permissions. How dare she try to keep my Keith from me!
Love's definition is division. It must be perpetually deconstructed,
I explained to him, when he came running, with a grin, this is how
it's always been. Love drives across cities, countries, worlds,
dimensions on a human engine, spitting up and out clouds
of platelets, billions of the little buggers, first on the scene
after a wound. The Creator's sexy, six-legged angels—
always invisible, but always hanging around, ready to hug.
After almost eighteen months, stranded on red clay, I found him,
cornered, kissed, whispered, and soon we resumed
the relationship we'd shared for two years as brother-sister-
lovers.*

*

Backwards, towards the slack words of cowards, two years
ago, I tried to spur third-party interest, put distance between
dysfunctional siblings. Georgia versus Newark. It didn't work,
not completely; she found me, aroused me ... Here's how we
always end: cold and wet, hardbodied, softwired, basking in
the unanswerable horrorglow.

*

*I lay dying, sufficient in the knowledge: There is no moral core
to the Love that exists in brisk waves and breezes on today's Earth,
burning on the fuel of a faith in the ephemeral. I don't even want to know,*

don't care to see, hear, or feel if either reaches into my robe,

takes my phone, searches and sees the text I sent

to Janet, drawing her here: "I know . . .

Let's meet and discuss like adults." Some insult,

I guess. She knew me in every way. But not that

me and her brother were better lovers.

The agony of hearing unsaid words, reading

faith in what appears to be its blood-opposite.

Let the two fake love as I take my questions

about what is true and false to a place where

the hues of love make sense, don't dye—

unlike the two rolling before my eyes,

on and off me, breaking

even more boundaries.

ABOUT THE AUTHOR

Harambee Grey-Sun is a poet and metaphysical/speculative fiction writer. The word best describing his work is "dark." He uses elements of fantasy, horror, noir, and science fiction to spin bizarre, mind-bending, and (some might say) heretical tales that explore the meaning of identity and the nature of consciousness. His poetry has appeared in a handful of literary journals, including *CrossConnect, Epicenter, RiverSedge,* the *South Carolina Review,* and the *Wisconsin Review.* He is also an alumnus of the Community of Writers at Squaw Valley.

FURTHER READING

Want to read more of the author's poetry?
Enter the HyperVerse: www.nextpoet.net